HOW THEY
LIVED

A MEDIEVAL
MONK

NIGEL HUNTER

Illustrated by
Edward Mortelmans

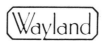

HOW THEY LIVED

Editor: Amanda Earl

First published in 1987 by
Wayland (Publishers) Limited
61 Western Road, Hove
East Sussex BN3 1JD, England

British Library Cataloguing in Publication Data
Hunter, Nigel
A medieval monk. – (How they lived)
Juvenile literature
I. Title   II. James, John, *1959—*   III. Series
255′.1′00942   BX3016
ISBN 0 85078 976 1

Typeset by Kalligraphics Limited, Redhill, Surrey
Printed and bound in Belgium by Casterman S.A.

CONTENTS

THE SOLEMN VOWS

The young man lay full-length before the altar, completely still. His body was draped in a black cloth. At his head and feet, single candleflames flickered. It was too late now for second thoughts. He had taken his vows to become a monk.

Lying there, with the solemn service continuing around him, he might have been dead. And in a way he was, for he could no longer be a part of the outside world. The church bell rang to signal his 'passing'.

Brother John, as he was now called, had sworn to live in the monastery for the rest of his life – to

As a sign of their religious devotion, most monks cut their hair around the crown. This ceremony was known as the 'tonsure'.

give up everything he owned, never to marry, and always to obey his superiors. At the word of the Abbot, he rose and went to take his place beside the other junior monks in the choir. The community had welcomed the new member to their Order. From now on, his life would be very different from the lives of ordinary men.

It was a scene that might have taken place almost anywhere in Britain during medieval times. In the year 1250, there were about a thousand monasteries scattered all over England, as well as many in Wales and Scotland. Some monasteries were large and wealthy, and others were very small. The number of monks in each monastery varied from perhaps a hundred to only five. Most monasteries were moderately well-off with about twenty monks.

In medieval Britain, monks belonged to one of several different Orders, each with its own special way of life. But, they all shared one common purpose – the worship and praise of the God of Christianity.

A MONASTIC LIFE

Brother John belonged to the Benedictine Order. It was the largest Order in England, with over 350 monasteries and 6,000 monks. The Benedictines were sometimes known as the Black Monks, because of the long black robes, or habits, they wore. Their way of life was based upon a code of conduct written by their founder, Saint Benedict (480–543). This was known as the *Rule of Saint Benedict*.

Under the Rule, the monastic day was divided into several parts. Most important was the time put by for communal public worship – altogether, about four hours. Another four hours were spent in

private prayer or study, and about six hours in domestic or manual work of some kind. The Rule laid great stress on obedience to the Abbot (who was considered to be the 'representative of Christ'). It also taught the importance of charity towards the poor, and hospitality for pilgrims, travellers and other guests.

In comparison with modern life, or everyday life in medieval times, life under the Benedictine Rule might seem very strict. Yet Saint Benedict was concerned that it should contain 'nothing harsh, nothing burdensome'. Some 'holy men' of his time lived in total solitude, with only the smallest amounts of food and drink. Compared with this, life for a Black Monk was relatively comfortable.

Although Benedictine monks led a very disciplined life, in their spare time they enjoyed fishing and working in the monastery gardens.

THE DIFFERENT ORDERS

The different Orders of monks could be distinguished quite easily by their dress. The Cluniacs wore fur-trimmed habits and they were famous for their elaborate and complex services performed in the most splendid churches. The Cistercians, in constrast to such lavishness, wore habits of undyed, whitish-grey cloth. They lived in very remote areas, particularly in Scotland and Wales, and they enjoyed simpler ceremonies. The Carthusians lived largely separate lives in their own individual cells. They ate very little food and wore rough canvas habits, with a hair shirt undergarment, which irritated the skin.

The Austins (Black Canons), Premonstratensians (White Canons) and the Gilbertines were all priests. They lived in small communities, but

DOMINICAN   KNIGHT TEMPLAR   FRANCISCAN

also visited the surrounding villages to preach and tend to the sick. Canons wore a surplice over their black habits and small caps. There were also communities of nuns belonging to the various orders. They too could be recognized by the different gowns and veils that they wore.

The Franciscans (Grey Friars), Dominicans (Black Friars) and Carmelites (White Friars) wore tunics with hoods and either grey, black or white cloaks. They preached in the towns and lived off the alms they were given. They travelled around a great deal, moving from one friary to another.

There were also the military monks, such as the Knights Templars and the Knights Hospitallers. They wore short tunics, and long cloaks bearing a black, white or red cross. They cared for the wounded in the Crusades, and sometimes even fought themselves.

Many of the different religious orders could be recognized by their dress. Most habits were quite plain.

CISTERCIAN   BENEDICTINE   CARTHUSIAN

9

A Typical Monastery

Most monasteries were very much alike. Brother John's was a typical example. It consisted of a group of inter-connected buildings, an area of well kept land, and a surrounding wall. It had been built in the twelfth century on land given to the monks by a rich feudal lord. The builders were local craftspeople, but there were also specialists in wood, stone, glass and metalwork who travelled around the country helping to build monasteries.

The central buildings were connected by courtyards, doorways, corridors and stairs. As the monks went about their everyday routine, they moved from place to place in a quiet, orderly fashion. Life was very organized, and everyone knew the

1. CHURCH
2. ABBOT'S HOUSE
3. CHAPTER HOUSE
4. DORMITORY
5. REFECTORY
6. LAVER
7. KITCHEN
8. INFIRMARY

rules. Conversation took place only at certain times, in certain places. The monastery was designed for worship, work and holy reading, so unnecessary talking was frowned upon.

Some of the monks were officials, with various special duties to perform. Each official was responsible for a specific part of the monastery. The Abbot was in charge overall. He was elected by the other monks, and stayed in office for life. The next most senior official was the Prior. These two were known as the 'father' and

Medieval craftsmen building an abbey.

'mother' of the community. Together, the monks formed a 'family'. There were also several paid servants in the monastery including porters, gardeners and cooks.

A typical medieval monastery. It was either called an abbey or a priory depending on whether it was run by an Abbot or a Prior.

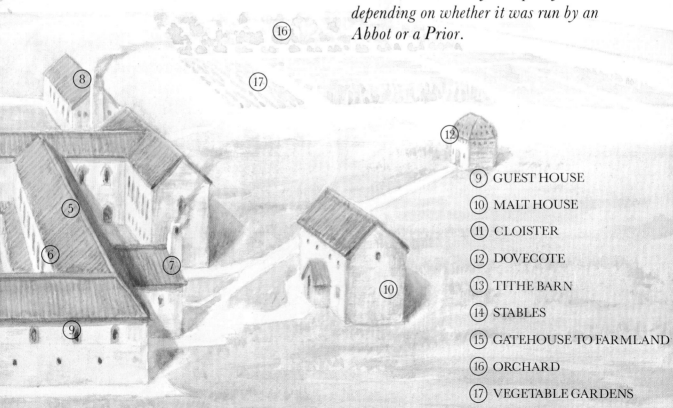

9 GUEST HOUSE
10 MALT HOUSE
11 CLOISTER
12 DOVECOTE
13 TITHE BARN
14 STABLES
15 GATEHOUSE TO FARMLAND
16 ORCHARD
17 VEGETABLE GARDENS

DAILY WORSHIP

Brother John's day was shaped by a regular pattern of church worship. Its main feature was a series of services called the *Divine Office* or *Hours*. There were seven of these – Matins, Prime, Terce, Sext, None, Vespers and Compline. The first took place soon after midnight and the last came just before sunset. They involved psalms, prayers and lessons.

There was also High Mass, which usually took place at about 10 a.m. As a junior, Brother John sometimes shared the task of handing out the prayer books and books of psalms to the other monks. High Mass was the most splendid service of the day. The church echoed with the monks voices, whose singing was led by the cantor. It was a form of music known as the *Gregorian chant*, and it is still

Service	Time of day
Start of monks' day Matins ————	Just after midnight 12 p.m.
Prime ————	At sunrise 6 a.m.
Terce ————	At 9 a.m.
Sext ————	Noon 12 a.m.
None ————	Mid afternoon 3 p.m.
Vespers ————	Early evening 6 p.m.
Compline ————	Sunset 7 p.m.

A table showing the different services in the monks' day. The times shown are approximate as exact times varied with the seasons.

one of the most beautiful reminders of the Middle Ages.

On certain days throughout the year, there were special services – at Advent, Christmas, Lent, Easter and Whitsuntide. There were also services dedicated to various saints. They involved ceremonial processions, with monks carrying banners

A stained-glass window in Canterbury Cathedral, showing monks in prayer.

Ordinary people were allowed to attend the monks' services. This is High Mass.

or even part of the remains of the body of a particular saint.

The church was the most important building in the monastery. It was richly decorated with stained-glass windows, carved screens, figure-sculptures and wall paintings. To the local people, who also attended many of the services, it seemed to hint of what Heaven must be like.

13

AT REST

Apart from those officials who had their own living-quarters, all the monks shared a common dormitory called the *dorter*. After Vespers and the service of Compline at sunset, the monks retired to bed at about 8 o'clock. Their night was divided into two periods of about four hours each. This was because they had to rise just after midnight for the service of Matins. For the monks, this was when each new day began.

The dorter was a long room with windows and beds evenly spaced on either side. Wooden panels between the beds gave each monk a certain amount of privacy. There was no furniture, except for the beds themselves and a mat on the floor. The monks slept on straw-filled mattresses, beneath rough woollen blankets. Their night-clothes were the same tunics that they wore during the day. When they went to bed, the monks simply took off their outer habits, shoes and stockings.

When they were woken by the bell for Matins, the first thing they did to start the new day was to 'cross'

themselves. Then they dressed, putting on special fur-lined night boots. These were not only warm on the cold stone floors, they were also quiet. Between sunset and dawn, the rules demanded more silence than usual. Six at a time, the monks would make their way into the church, with

Opposite *Monks leave their dormitory for the service of Matins.*
Below *Monks attending one of the many services held during the day.*

one of the juniors leading the way with a lantern. No doubt they were very pleased, an hour or two later, to return to the dorter to catch up on their sleep!

In the early hours of the morning, at sunrise, they were woken once again for the service of Prime.

BUSINESS AND DISCIPLINE

Every morning the monks gathered together to consider the day-to-day affairs of their community. This meeting took place in one of the monastery's most impressive buildings – the Chapter House. As usual everything followed a set pattern. The juniors entered first, and then the older, senior monks. They stood by their seats until the Abbot arrived, and as he passed them they bowed respectfully. Then, to show their faithfulness to the vow of obedience, one of the seniors kissed the Abbot's hand.

All of the monks met in the monastery's Chapter House to talk about the day-to-day running of their community.

A medieval illuminated picture depicts a Chapter meeting.

After this, one of the juniors read out loud from a book which listed down all the names of the different saints. From this, they were given the name of the saint or martyr they would commemorate the next day. Then came the main business of the meeting. Any monk could stand up and speak about anything he thought needed changing or correcting. If someone had something to confess, he did so there and then. Those monks who were not carrying out their duties properly were also named.

Discipline was strict. Light punishment included a diet of bread and water, or a beating with a birch-rod. But more serious offences could be punished with a whole year of solitary confinement in chains. Any monk who betrayed his religious vows would, of course, be expelled from the monastery.

This beautiful Chapter House at Salisbury Cathedral, built between 1263–1284, clearly shows it was one of the monastery's most impressive buildings.

HOLY STUDIES

At the centre of the monastery there was an important area called the *cloister*. Apart from the church, this was where the monks spent most of their time. It consisted of a grass-covered square bordered with flowers, and four roofed 'walks' running around it. Large arched windows on the inner walls of each walk provided plenty of light, and elaborate doorways at each corner led to the other monastery buildings.

It was mainly used during two parts of the day. Firstly, there was the time between the Chapter meeting and High Mass in the morning; and secondly, there was the afternoon, when most of the monks' studying was done.

The northern walk was where the senior monks worked. Each had a finely carved workplace called a *carrel*, which was set into the wall. Here they could study in peace and away from draughts. The carrels had enough room for a desk and some books. Other books were stored in cupboards in the corridors.

Brother John and his fellow juniors worked in the western walk of the cloister. The novice monks (those who had not yet taken their vows) worked in the opposite eastern walk. For the novices and juniors, it was rather like being at school. Senior monks taught them the Holy Scriptures, and gave lessons about the monastic way of life. They also practised reading out loud and singing. Altogether, the cloister was the busiest part of the monastery.

Opposite *The Abbot instructs a group of monks in the cloister.*

Below *This twelfth-century picture shows a novice monk in holy studies.*

FOOD AND DRINK

Every day after High Mass, the monks went to the refectory, or *frater*, for dinner. Sometimes this was their only meal. But during the summer months they ate again in the evening, and those in poor health were often given an extra ration of fresh bread soaked in beer. The monks' dinner consisted of two cooked dishes, generally beans, eggs, cheese, pastry and vegetables in various combinations, plus bread and beer. Wine and mead was usually drunk and the meal finished with fresh fruit. On Fridays, the monks always ate fish, and, on special occasions, there was chicken, pork and spicy cakes.

Each week one of the juniors was appointed to read to the others during the meal. This was an important task, and he had to prepare his chosen passage carefully. If it happened to be Brother John, then he knew that the following week he would be one of the servers. Four juniors served the meals to the others. They had to take great care with the dishes, 'not running or jumping' as the Rule stated. The monks had to eat with 'the greatest modesty' and politeness. If a monk spilt any food he had to take 'penance' in the middle of the room until called back by the Prior.

When the meal was finished, the leftovers were collected to be given to the poor. After saying Grace, the monks departed, singing a psalm. Then came a second meal, for the reader, the servers and the cooks.

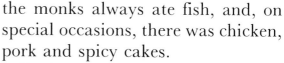

Left *Monks enjoyed drinking wine or mead with their meal.*

A typical mealtime in a medieval monastery. While some junior monks served, another was chosen to read a religious lesson during the meal.

RECREATION AND WORK

The afternoon began with a period of rest and recreation. During the longer days of summer, the monks relaxed in the dormitory for an hour. During the winter months, the seniors were often invited to the Abbot's lodging to enjoy a glass of wine. Meanwhile, if the weather was fine, the juniors, novices and their masters went into the monastery garden for a game of bowls, or some other light-hearted exercise. On cold, rainy days they could go to the *calefactory*, or warming-room, where a fire was kept alight. Otherwise, they would play games like chess in

In the summer afternoons, many of the monks would work at harvesting crops in the monastery's fields.

the cloister.

After the service of None, came the main period of work and study. Most went to the cloister to work at their books and lessons. Others – the officials and their assistants – spent much of this time on their own special tasks. Tending to the unkeep of the monastery buildings, including the furniture, the altar goods, and cooking equipment all took time. Sometimes the whole community went into the fields belonging to the monastery to work on the crops.

Some of the monks were highly skilled craftsmen and artists. Their work was on show throughout the monastery – on carved wooden screens, decorative panelling, stone-carving and beautiful stained-glass windows. All this and more was done for 'the glory of God'.

When they had time to themselves, monks sometimes went to the workshop. Many were skilled artists and much of their beautiful stone-carving and stained-glass work was on show.

BOOKS AND THE SCRIPTORIUM

Books were a most important feature of monastic life. There were the holy books kept for use in church, and for private study, books about the lives of the saints, books by the classical writers of Ancient Greece and Rome and records and documents of all kinds.

Books were written, as well as read, in the monastery. The *scribes*, or writers, worked in a room above the Chapter House, called the *scriptorium*. It would be many years before the junior monks were allowed into this room.

A scribe works in the scriptorium on an illuminated book.

Some of the scribes spent years composing their own original work. Others specialized in illustration. But most were mainly occupied with copying. This was a slow, painstaking task, but in the days before printing was invented, it was the only way books could be reproduced. The quantity of books produced was quite small, but since few people outside the monasteries could read or write, that hardly mattered. Their quality was extremely high.

All the books were beautiful works of art. They were written on

A detail of an illumination, showing the skill of the monks' work.

A beautiful page from a medieval book completed by Benedictine monks.

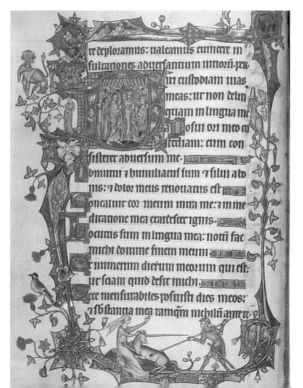

parchment with goose-quill pens, and the text was decorated with 'illuminations'. These were large, delicately painted initial letters, and brightly-coloured border designs. The illustrations often filled whole pages. They were done with paints the monks prepared from a variety of natural substances and plants. Dyes and paints were also specially brought over from Europe for such work. Many designs were gilded with gold leaf. The books were bound in fine leather, their covers sometimes inlaid with precious stones. All books were fastened with an attractive metal clasp.

25

HEALTHCARE

About every twelve weeks, each monk was given a curious medical treatment called 'blood-letting'. This involved having a vein opened, and a certain amount of blood drawn off. It was a common belief at the time that blood contained a portion of 'bad humours', which could be taken out in this way. This did at least give the monks a break from the normal routine. It involved a visit to the infirmary building or *farmery*, followed by three days' rest, with rather more food than usual.

Medieval medicine included a strange treatment called 'blood-letting'.

Friars travelled around the villages and towns helping the sick.

In general, the monks were very healthy compared with ordinary folk in medieval Britain. Fresh running water from a nearby stream, and good plumbing in the toilets (the *necessarium*) and the washing-room (the *laver*), led to a high standard of hygiene. If they ever did fall ill, they were cared for in the farmery. This building had its own kitchen and chapel.

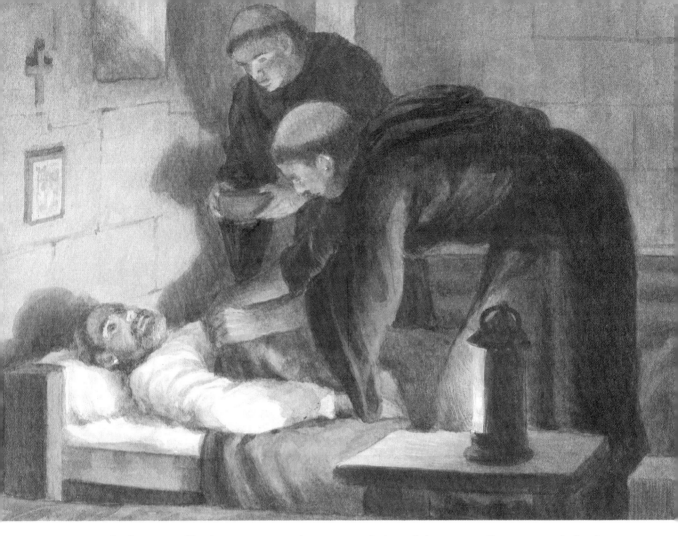

When monks became ill, they were cared for in the monastery's farmery. Here, they were given mostly herbal medicines, which were specially made.

The *infirmarian*, who looked after the patients, made sure the farmery was always clean and warm. Under Benedictine Rule he had to be a gentle, kind man, who treated the sick and the elderly with great sympathy. He was an expert in herbal medicine, mixing his cures from special plants grown in the *herbarium*.

Some illnesses of course could not be cured. Whenever one of the Brothers was about to die, the whole community was called upon, and the monk was given his 'last rites'. After death, he was laid in the church overnight and all the monks gathered alongside to pray. The following day he would be buried in the monastery's well-kept cemetery.

27

TRAVELLERS AND PILGRIMS

Very often, monks would see strangers in the monastery. It was a basic rule that guests should be received 'as if they were Christ Himself'. This applied to the poor as much as to the rich, to women as well as men, and to ordinary folk – merchants, travellers and pilgrims – as well as to monks from other monasteries. The most important guests stayed in the Abbot's lodging. The poorest, including beggars and wandering lepers, were given food, shelter and often clothing. They stayed in the monastery's Charity House or *almonry*.

Most visitors, however, were looked after by the guest-master, or *hospitarius* as he was called. They stayed in special rooms which were

Medieval Monasteries provided food, shelter and hospitality for travelling pilgrims.

always ready. Guests were given as much food as they wanted and spent time talking to the monks. They were allowed to attended some of the monks' religious services. Servants were also looked after and any horses would be cared for too.

Most guests stayed for about two days, but if by chance they felt ill, they were welcome to stay longer. When they eventually left, they showed their gratitude by giving whatever money they could afford.

One other type of guest was much more rare – a person fleeing from the

Important guests who visited the monastery stayed with the Abbot in his lodgings.

law. He or she was allowed to take 'sanctuary' in the church, and was safe from those who pursued them. After confessing the crime and swearing obedience to the Abbot, the fugitive was allowed to stay in the monastery for forty days. Then, after appearing before a magistrate, they would go to the nearest port (carrying a wooden cross in their hand) and sail away into exile.

THE END OF THE OLD LIFE

Between the sixth and sixteenth centuries, English monasteries grew and prospered. But, during the reign of Henry VIII, they were unmercifully suppressed. The monks were forced out of their monasteries and the buildings with their contents were either destroyed or sold to the King's supporters. There were many reasons for this. One was the belief that the religious standards of the monks had declined – that they were living in idle luxury. The major reason, however, seems to be King Henry's own need for money to pay off his enormous debts.

Very little remains of the medieval monasteries today. Certain churches used by the monks remain, but most are just tumble-down ruins. Some books, and the monks' beautiful craftsmanship can be seen in museums, but most have been lost forever.

As for Brother John and his fellow monks – if their religious beliefs were true, they now rank 'next below the saints and Apostles in Heaven'.

Rievaulx Abbey, Yorkshire. Today, such ruins can only give us a glimpse of what life was like for a medieval monk.

GLOSSARY

Alms Gifts of money and goods given to the poor or needy.

Apostles The first followers of Christ, also known as his disciples.

Community A group of people living together.

Crusades Religious wars fought by the Christians against the Muslims from 1095–1272, in the hope of recapturing the Holy Land.

Divine Office The daily prayers recited by those in a religious order.

Dormitory A large bedroom with many beds.

Exile Banishment from one's country and being forced to live abroad.

Feudal Medieval social system, whereby the land was owned by supporters of the King.

Friary A monastery run by Friars.

Fugitive A person running away from capture or harm.

Grace Prayer of thanks for a meal.

Hospitality To offer friendship and accommodation to visitors.

Last rites A religious ceremony performed when someone is close to death.

Leper A person with the disease leprosy, usually treated as outcasts in Medieval times.

Martyr Someone who suffers or dies for their beliefs.

Medieval Relating to the Middle Ages (from the fifth to the fifteenth century).

Monastery A place where monks live, also known as an 'abbey' or a 'priory', depending on the rank of the superior in charge (an Abbot or a Prior).

Order Religious group with its own particular rules.

Parchment Good quality, strong paper, originally made of sheep or goatskin.

Penance A religious act of prayer to ask forgiveness.

Procession A large number of people proceeding in a line.

Recreation Enjoyable exercise or occupation.

Ritual A custom or ceremony.

Sanctuary To take shelter in a church at a time of personal danger and be safe from pursuers.

Surplice A loose white garment worn by members of the church.

MORE BOOKS TO READ

G. Caselli, *The Everyday life of a Medieval Monk*, (Macdonald, 1986)

S. Hadenius and B. Janrup, *A Medieval Monastery*, (Lutterworth Press, 1980)

P. Davies, *Growing up in the Middle Ages*, (Wayland, 1972)

A. and B. Steel, *The Middle Ages*, (Wayland, 1986)

R. J Unstead, *The Middle Ages*, (A&C Black, 1974)

INDEX

Picture acknowledgements
The pictures in this book were supplied by the following: Aerofilms 30; Aldus Archive 17 (left), 26 (right); The Bodleian Library 18, 25 (both); The British Library (HR 179a) 4, (Ms. Cott. Dom. AXVII, f.122v) 14; Mary Evans Picture Library 11; Michael Holford 17 (right), 28; Sonia Halliday Picture Library 12. The rest of the pictures belong to Wayland Picture Library. The artwork on page 12 is by Malcolm S. Walker.